Tulips for Dad

Richard Brown
Illustrated by Cliff Wright

CAMBRIDGE

When I was three-and-a-half years old, my dad
made a wooden wheelbarrow for me. He painted
it bright green. Inside it, he put a little trowel
and a pair of wooden shears. The shears went
"snip-snip, snip-snip."

I loved messing about in our garden. I had
a little patch of ground where I could dig holes
with my trowel. I loved to snip at leaves with
my shears. My dad said that I would make
a good gardener.

The man next door liked gardening too.
He mowed his lawn and dug up weeds. He grew
flowers everywhere. He loved his flowers.

I liked the way he hummed to himself.

I spent a lot of time watching the man next door.
I tried to copy the way that he dug with his trowel.
I watched the way that he snipped with his shears.

He would say, "Hello, Margaret. Are you
having a good time?"

On the other side of the fence, there was
a row of tulips. They grew tall and proud.

I could just touch these tulips through the fence. Their heads were like bright red cups. "Beautiful, aren't they?" said the man next door.

One day I filled my wheelbarrow with grass cuttings. I thought to myself, "I want Daddy to see this." I ran inside, calling, "Daddy, Daddy."

But my mum put her finger to her lips and said, "Daddy's not feeling very well. He's having a rest upstairs. You've got to be very quiet."

I wandered about the garden for a bit. I was feeling sad for my dad.

Then I remembered that when people are ill, you can cheer them up by giving them flowers. I wanted to cheer my dad up.

I stared at the tulips in next-door's garden.
Then I had an idea.

I put my shears into my wheelbarrow and
I wheeled it round the fence into next-door's
garden. There was no-one there.

The tulips were very tall.

"Snip-snip, snip-snip," went my little wooden shears. I snipped off the heads of every one of those tulips, except for one that I couldn't quite reach. (Well, I was only three-and-a-half.)

I took my wheelbarrow of tulip heads to our front door. "Knock-knock, knock-knock." Mum answered the door. She did look surprised. "What *have* you done, Margaret?" she said.

"I've brought some flowers for Daddy," I said.
"They're to help him get better."

But my mum didn't seem at all pleased.
"Oh dear," she said, "oh dear, oh dear."

I pulled out a big handful of tulip heads and said, "Shall I take them up to Daddy?"

But Mum said, "Oh, you naughty girl. What *am* I going to tell the man next door?"

I didn't know why Mum was angry. "Tell him they're for Daddy," I said with a big smile.

Mum took the tulip heads from me. I wonder what she did with them.

Later, we had to go to see the man next door. While Mum was saying to him, "I'm very, very sorry," I was looking at the one last tulip that was left.

It waved about on a lovely long stalk. I asked loudly, "Can I have *that* tulip for Daddy?"

Mum tried to hush me up. But the man smiled
and said to me, "You take it, love. I'm sure it'll
make your dad feel better."

I climbed upstairs with the tulip and gave it
to Daddy. At first he smiled. Then he laughed.

Then he got up. My tulip must have made him
feel better. I was so glad that I'd given it to him.

But the funny thing was that, after that day,
I never could find my little wooden shears.
I wonder what happened to them.